THE LOST THOUGHTS

LOSING HOPES ALWAYS IS THE STEP TO RUNNING YOURSELF

WILVIA DSOUZA

Contents

ONE

WHAT IS LOVE?

Love,
A desire to be with someone.
Individuals who commit to each other for a long time.
Sense of longing, passion, care, and dream.

Words cannot describe the tenderness of love,
The true meaning will be revealed with time and action.

Love is when everyone you care about loves you regardless of your size, colour, shape, or gender.

The greatest sign of love is the ability to be angry at your loved ones and return to them as new.

Love can be in a form of feeling, necessity or just time pass.

It can feel like a fairy-tale to a child.
It can alleviate loneliness for adults.
In the eyes of the young, it's just profit or loss.

When a lover experiences it, it is the best thing that could

happen to them.
Trust and loyalty are the cornerstones of a man's character.

Commitment and gain are the basis for a woman's motivation.

Mothers often sacrifice for their children.

Fathers can see it as a duty.
Power can be a concern for a brother.
An egotistical nerd may see it as a waste of time.

It can be a means of passing
g the time for a pervert.
Theists can consider it a belief.
Logic can be the answer for an atheist.

For a philosopher, it is something to think about.

And the list goes on.
Love doesn't have a clear definition or meaning it depends on the person and how they feel.

Love can be relaxing and beautiful.
Love can be toxic and manipulative.
Love can be giving and taking.
Love can be a fantasy or a romcom drama.

Love can be at first sight for some.
Love can be from hatred to liking someone.

In the end, love is manifested by gripping out of your comfort zone and letting the other person know you care.

Or,

Love is a strong positive feeling that makes you feel safe via Self-love

TWO

IN THE END, I WISH YOU THE BEST

I took an arrow to my heart
though I knew it was a red flag.

Mustered up hopes,
Never cheated or prevaricated

Many a time thought of,
turning back the clock and making it right.

Standing on the edge of the water,
wrote a fight song to gather my courage.

Gathered my courage,
ended up being a bad liar.

Went back to the zone of 'smooth like butter'

but ignited like a Dynamite.

Things were getting out of hand,
but everything I needed was for you to understand.

The more I silenced,
the more I thought as it was our last.

I knew it all way round,
this was only going to hurt.

But still swallowed up,
to give you chances to be a pioneer.

Used others as a shield to cover up feelings,
but ended up realising my true feelings.

Started with the pattern of fake love,
ended up being a sucker for you.

Developed the imagination of a thousand years,
but the closure was just a dream.

It took longer to let go,
but still, I would have taken the same road I took afore.

I can't help you anymore, that's why,
In the end, I wish you the best.

THREE

LOVE; WITH THE WRONG PERSON

Took a break from love,
but didn't know there would be a twist.

Well, got to know this one would surpass,
all the other love stories of mine.

This was toxic and manipulative,
So, gave in to let me try.

The feeling was good but unacceptable,
Because the twist was down the road of many challenges.

It didn't take long for me to understand,
this was it that I wanted for so long.

There were heartbeats, butterflies and chills down my spine,
There was love and hate but in a very seductive slot.

This wasn't a true love genre,
but a soulmate genre.

Love lets you notice the scent of your partner,
So, did I.

Well, oh well, I grew hard in love,
That meant the whole world.

Nothing seemed more attractive than,
Just that person.

This time, I was in love,
But with the wrong person.

FOUR

Heartbreak; Unforgettable Ashes

Love lured them into the evil spell
Cast another spell of hatred
A destructive emotion held in
Didn't show it until it developed
The painful truth,
No one to turn to
An unintentional punitive act,
Never will the spell be lifted
Until these ashes are swept away.

FIVE

IF IT'S YOU, I WILL EMBRACE IT

Throbbing heart,
Even if I have no idea, why?

The mind stops me.
Taking away the one that I want.

Body reacts.
Regardless, of the thousand hate words, I say about you.

Lips respond,
The truth hurts me, but I hope you won't mind hearing it.

Eyes closed,
This keeps me thinking about you even more while I try to forget those moments.

I see myself as a mirror of duality.
The mere sight of you causes me to feel nothing
And, I miss you when I am not with you.

Perhaps I do not want to reveal how I feel to you.

My thoughts keep on pestering me to run away.
But I keep getting dragged the further I go.

Could it be karma or fate?
Or, Shall I take it as a blessing?

The saying goes,
Our body never lies, regardless of what the words say.
Our eyes never lie, no matter how much our bodies may lie.

There are times when I wish this was a dream.
There are times when I want to pause and enjoy the moment.
My aversion to getting close to people comes from the feeling that it is meaningless.

It's a feeling I hate.
If it, is you, I will embrace it?

SIX

Poisoned to Feelings of Ignorance

Someday just someday
I could discern it kindly

The profoundly relished that you shared
The trust you bestowed

No matter how much incognisant they were
Hope life has given you the moment you wanted

An awakening

A clear heart and mind to perceive the light
Through the narrow path of your recognizance

Time again, you must have hoped to go back
To rectify it

Time again, you hurt them

Hope you could perceive the incipient light
Just like the light, you found years ago

Endeavoured so hard to get over
Wondered,
What was the desire you felt?

Back in the days, you conceived it as an illusion
When time went by
It transpired,

My heart commenced recognising the moment
Even when you could not reach out to them

You questioned, manipulated yourself,
You let them burn in it the fire you initiated
Now nor your tears could calm those flames down

They wronged you
They used you

What was more consequential to you?
Drifted from your fingers
Like the sand slipping away lifelessly

You must have strived to get over it

Thought,
This world would not even accept you as you are.

Still lost in those phrenic conceptions, endeavouring to

decipher

Why were you so nescient?

Hope life could give you another chance to revive
Seemed akin, it was too vigorous for you to survive

Fate never showed you the Sign
It felt like a surprise to feel our hearts align

You could not accept the fate
That is why you turned your back to hate

But there is no going back now
Enslaved to the same fate

Consummate the voyage
Relinquish the one you desired
And clear the storm you once started.

SEVEN

HOPE WE COULD STILL BE IN EACH OTHER'S HEART

Someday just someday
I could discern it kindly
The profoundly relish that you shared
The trust you bestowed
No matter how much incognisant they were
Hope life has given you the moment you wanted
An awakening
A clear heart and mind to perceive the light
Through the narrow path of your incognizance
Time again, you must have hoped to go back
To rectify it
Time again, you hurt them

Hope you could perceive the incipient light
Just like the light, you found years ago
Endeavoured so hard to get over

Wondered,
What was the desire you felt?
Back in the days, you conceived it as an illusion
When time went by
It transpired,
My heart commenced recognising the moment
Even when you could not reach out to them
You questioned, manipulated yourself,
You let them burn in it the fire you initiated
Now nor your tears could calm those flames down

They wronged you
They used you
What was more consequential to you?
Drifted from your fingers
Like the sand slipping away lifelessly
You must have strived to get over it
Thought,
This world would not even accept you as you are.
Still lost in those phrenic conceptions, endeavouring to decipher
Why were you so nescient?
Hope life could give you another chance to revive
Seemed akin, it was too vigorous for you to survive
Fate never showed you the Sign
It felt like a surprise to feel our hearts align
You could not accept the fate
That is why you turned your back to hate
But there is no going back now
Enslaved to the same fate
Consummate the voyage
Relinquish the one you desired
And clear the storm you once started

EIGHT

A REASON TO SMILE AGAIN

Tons of pain in my heart, but I still don't lend any occasion for any twinge to annex me,
For they have a very strong deterrent and that's my smile,
No matter how much miffed, gloomy, shattered I am,
Still, I'll never let my smile tail off.

It gives me a purpose to overcome my distress,
Poise to tackle the reality,
And an urge to accomplish an concluded voyage,
A smile is which tells me to take no notice of 'a big cheese',
Trying to judge me and preside over me.

A companion who I may quit on when obscurity invades,
Yet it never forsakes me.
What would I be without my apron?
When I am discomfited before my folks and
Have no tactic to look towards them and dusk spreads,

Yet there is a jiff of hope to smile and I do it without any

gaucheness.
Love is smashed to smithereens, trust is growing fainter,
I sense nothing other than numbness

Nevertheless, I have all the reason to smile again.

NINE

MY SWEET DEAR: LOVE TALE

Shiny suns depict your smile in all its glory.
You captivate me with your sparkling eyes, with the world of your land.

Wonder, what was it that made me feel, so soft towards you?

Soft touches accentuate the living sculpture's beauty.
The warmth of belonging is tasted on the lips,
The light of the moment brightens its essence.

Passing by me, I find it hard to breathe.
Cherry blossoms glisten on the cheeks, transforming their colour into the fruity extract of
strawberries,
Your smile hides behind those hungry eyes you flash as you look at me.

The frozen instance, at the moment, while brushing past me,

A sweet sensation, "how shall I describe this?"
Touching the silky feel of your skin and smelling the sweet scent from you're somatic.
Breaking the barriers and seeking attention with your eyes.
Signifying, only the person who makes your heart flutter can lift your bridal serape.

What can be said about those beautiful eyes that expressed so many emotions without any
words?

My sweet dear, we have a love story that can only be treasured by the closed pages of time.

TEN

LOVE IT IS: WHAT WOULD YOU NAME ALL OF THESE.

LOVE! What a scenic sensation to feel;
That skip of beat when you gaze towards the one you love,
The yearning to be with,
The touch, which bewitched,
The bond you feel when you are close at hand,
Audacity to face every hurdle
Those mesmerizing eye's gawping their way to grasp attention,
Grin, which makes you woozy,
The song, which clutches you to A Fantasy Realm,
The graze, you cannot resist.
Those late-night night talks, which make you, feel like a doofus,
How can you blank over on those petite clashes that drew

you closer,
To the one you love.
Those compromises you made keeping aside your ego.
The words buried underneath your lips tussling their way out
Yet, you hide it so that you would not hurt,
Those gifts bought just for your smile,
Made the day go delightful
The time spent in silence was incredibly
Charming and exquisite
Love it is. What would you name all of these?

ELEVEN

SUCCESS & CHOICES

Leaving our mother's womb, we took our first step.
Shadowed by our parents,
Making decisions for us about what is right and erroneous

The second step is for us to decide for ourselves
By verbalizing with our parents what is precise and just,
To obviate ourselves from facing unknown challenges.

Thirdly, we opiate arduous paths because we are discombobulated.
Moreover, no one can exhort us.
At times, we might doubt ourselves.

A sense of accomplishment and wings of liberation comes with the last step
We choose what fits our habits and needs.
It's either to forget the first step or to take the path we feel is right.

It's all up to us,
The right,
The erroneous,
The culls,
The road.

At the terminus, we just need to accomplish something.

TWELVE

I HEAR THE 'SONG OF HEAVEN'

As I stand at the edge of the cliff,
I am eagerly awaiting the sound of the angels' song in heaven.

I see a red flower passing by
Giving, it's a way for me to capture it.

Shaken by the sudden darkness,
reaching the soft layer of the flower.

My soul is blinded by the hope of love and freedom,
The sinful journey was put on hold.

Captivated by the beauty and serenity of the red flower,
I danced to its tune.

Enchanted by the beauty and sweetness of the red flower.
I Embraced, the journey to the end of a disheartening voyage.

It was a journey of fun, excitement and mystery.

Heart thumping, eyes dilating, body tied down.
Possessed by the red flower spirit.

A half-real mind in ‘its’ world.
I scream, calling its name.

The mind stopped, eyes turned white, body lifeless.
I hear the angels singing the song of heaven.

THIRTEEN

TEARS ON MY PILLOW

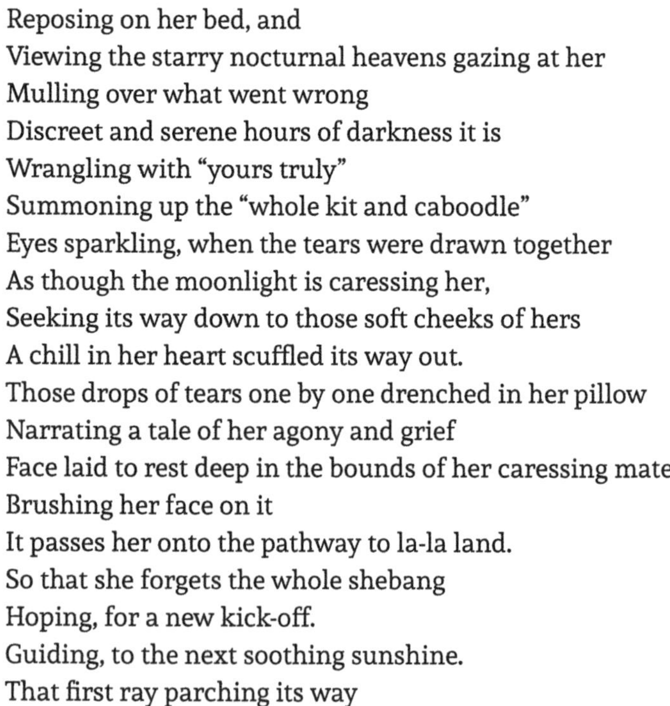

Reposing on her bed, and
Viewing the starry nocturnal heavens gazing at her
Mulling over what went wrong
Discreet and serene hours of darkness it is
Wrangling with "yours truly"
Summoning up the "whole kit and caboodle"
Eyes sparkling, when the tears were drawn together
As though the moonlight is caressing her,
Seeking its way down to those soft cheeks of hers
A chill in her heart scuffled its way out.
Those drops of tears one by one drenched in her pillow
Narrating a tale of her agony and grief
Face laid to rest deep in the bounds of her caressing mate
Brushing her face on it
It passes her onto the pathway to la-la land.
So that she forgets the whole shebang
Hoping, for a new kick-off.
Guiding, to the next soothing sunshine.
That first ray parching its way

Moreover, making her deem;
"Nothing happened the other day".

FOURTEEN

CHANGES; WHEN IT COMES TO LOVE

I'm changing, I can't remember who I was.
When I don't have you nearby.
Oh, and I'm not sure how I'll survive.

But I want to love somebody.
Love somebody like you.

I'm letting go of all my loneliness, yesterday.
I've forgiven myself for the mistakes I've made.
Now there's just one thing, the only thing.

Yeah, I want to feel the sunshine.
Shining down on me and you.
When you put your arms around me.
You let me know there's nothing in this world I can't do.
I want to love somebody like you.

I’m changing, and I'm not sure how I’ll survive without you.

FIFTEEN

IT'S NOT LOVE, IT'S INFATUATION

The scent of seduction.
In a way that cannot be described, it is beautiful.
Our minds are rebelling.
What drives us to be so obsessed?
A clash of selfish motives and the point of confusion ensued.

Smitten by the undeniable lust, surely hellhound.
As they get nearer to someone else, go paranoid.
Love, attraction, or Like; Irreplaceable memories.
Get the feeling in motion by rewinding the thoughts.

Observing their actions. Looked at them briefly.
Their sweat drips when they are close
To grab their attention, create a sense of craziness.
An everlasting feeling and wanting to be in front of those you love.

Trying to get in their way.

Clenching your fist as they smile at you.
Accepting whatever they say with ease.
Fantasying about unreal scenarios and avoiding reality.

Being with them makes every moment better
During their absence, feel emptiness.

Making us believe it's real by using our imagination.
It's not love, It's infatuation.

SIXTEEN

INFATUATED SEDUCTION

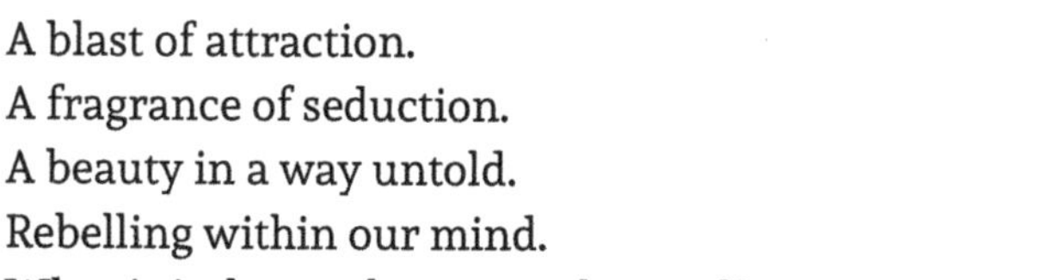

A blast of attraction.
A fragrance of seduction.
A beauty in a way untold.
Rebelling within our mind.
What is it that makes us so obsessed?
Selfish motives with the pinch of confusion clashed.

Hell bound while thinking about the undeniable lust.
Paranoid while they get closer to someone else.
Attraction, like or love: Irreplaceable memories.
Rewinding the thoughts of getting the feeling in action.

Eyes observe the activities they carry out.
Sweat dripping while they are close
A sense of craziness to grab their attention.
Feeling everlasting and ones whom you want to be in front of.

Trying to get in the way they go through.

Clenching your fist while they smile at you.
Easily agreeing to whatever they say.
Avoiding the reality and fantasizing about the unreal scenario.
Using our own imagination and making us think it's real.
It's not love, It's infatuation.

SEVENTEEN

LIFE IS NOTHING BUT A GAME

It takes time to settle on what's right and wrong.
Growing older, we become more aware of the stages of the drama,
With close ones, sometimes
at times, with ourselves.

Our thoughts about life and loving ourselves
Fades away slowly.
A feeling of numbness sets in, and you feel like hiding.
The greed of people disgusts you, yet you are compelled to follow the same path.

Dirt always drags you to hell no matter how much you say no,
Associated with them is not what you want.
Your forced smile will not work,
while sadness holds sway.

Comfort zones you've always cherished won't embrace you,

Slowly, your emotions become furious.
You never again experience happiness, again.
Confidence will start eroding.

Although the years pass, you know that the future is not yours.
Death awaits, and your accomplishment fades.
Emotions have no value.
Likewise, our lives are just games at different levels.

EIGHTEEN

THE TWINS OF THE WORDS LANGUAGE OF DEEPENING SOLITUDE

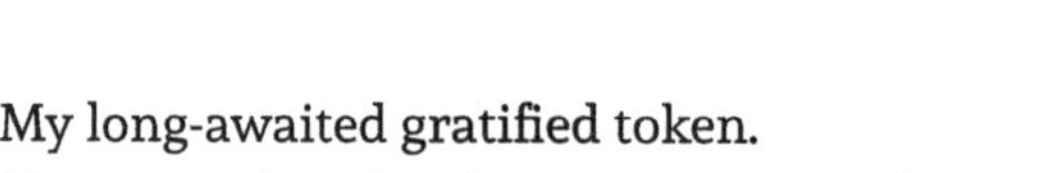

My long-awaited gratified token.
Heart convinced to the mystery unspoken.
Filled with passion, filled with grace.
Untold integrity, which is never misplaced.

Showered a bounty onto the treacherous.
How to explain a moment insalubrious.
Steps intact to the cautious well-being.
Mocked to the presence of foreseeing.

Pain overflowing without mercy.

Shall not I turn my back and fancy?
The truth they shout, the truth they whisper.
Close your ears and reverse your thinker.

The laborious path overshadows pure pride.
It said, 'rest assured and rules abide.'
'Focus on winning, focus on light.'
'Keep everything aside and let go of the fright.'

Innocent sweats carve their way.
Quivering at the powerless, the rich are unswayed.
Work on your confidence and perch for redemption.
There is no place for your stereotypical assumptions.

Slaved to the illiberal 'shadowed' salvage.
Everybody is enslaved to the reluctant bondage.
Conceal your sorrows deep down into your lecherous mind.
Bind your soul to purity and never shall you be pined.

Sleuth your thoughts in two parts.
One to linger positively, and another to regard it as art.
Shaken by the thought of disbelief.
Gather your strength and subsist 'a sigh of relief.'

NINETEEN

HEARTLESS SOUL THE MOCKERY OF THE PEACEFUL WORLD

Reminiscing about the departed memories,
I Fled with the rush of the waterfall in mind.
Back to the days of tranquillity and frolicsomeness.
Smiling at one another without hesitation.

Harnessing the frenetic concept of once again living that life.
But it's too tardy as the days pass by.
You know everyone has developed countenances to shield themselves.
And nobody would lend their hands to anyone.

Visualisation of a tranquil world, but we can't maintain ourselves.

Parallel to the wonderland lies the land of hell.
Swayed to the unruliest thing, life never mattered.
Hush to the grungy works, while you speak up, you stuttered.

Tears flowed from the eyes of the life-giver.
Ruthlessly turn your back.
Bowed in the act of munificence,
Shattered, until picked, the broken shard.

Ran towards everyone for a piece of advice.
They said: never to trust anyone.
In the world of falsehoods and deception,
It seemed more comfortable not to breathe.

People vociferate about diversity and tranquillity.
The world whispers to you; you live in hell.
Knock... Knock...
Inner self interprets; you are in hell.

It appears that Pandora's box has been opened again.
The deities of ravage have decided their course of action.
There is no choice for mankind.
Until the cries of pain are heard by justice.

Slew the words of all the holy books.
It contains recreational tranquil land.
Laugh at us anyway,
We picked the flower of havoc and end.

Turned to the light that brightened each time the wrath arose.
With bloody hands and a heartless soul,

Smiled travestying at the divine light.
Until the light turned to colour on the hands of the satanic soul.

The smile faded when the king of hell made its way to the surface.
A scream of inculpable prayer reached the ears of the soil they were lying on.
Fated to God's wrath, the earth embraced the dying souls.
Mock yourself now, for you disturbed the quietude above.

Heartless soul, inculpable prayers, ruthless demeanour.
Let me tell you, all three are signs of avarice.
When I contemplate violence and torture,
I recollect the visual, the scene of hell where people are burned and slashed.

TWENTY

REMEMBER THE FIRST LESSON YOU LEARNT

Taking a stroll, along the river.
I gaze at my reflection.
Sometimes with empathy and sometimes with hatred.
Deciding on what to do next.

Is it wise to go with the flow?
Like the flow of water down the mountainside
Or, Could I build a dam to control the water in my mind?

As the days pass, the flow grows stronger.
As it rains heavily, I am unable to flee.
Is it wise to take advantage of the branches that are lending a hand?
Or, It's up to me to take on the challenges coming ahead.

Stronger and stronger is the current,

Over the misery, the moon shows off its radiance.
I don't know what is happening, but the waves hit my face.
It takes me back to where I was strolling.

Seeing the moment clearly.
Touching my face gently, I smile.
I was strewed with water;
Learning two things from myself.
One, Believe in yourself, whether you are alone or not.
Two, Remember the first lesson you learned.

TWENTY-ONE
ACROSTIC

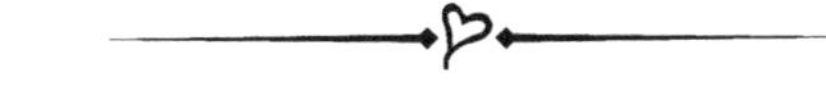

HEARTS

Heard your voice from afar
Eager to meet your miles apart
Ardent to Love you one more time
Reaching out to your hands
Trying to break the shackles
Screaming amid the painful strive.

♡♡♡

TOUCH

Thirst, which never Quenches
Oath, which never Succeeds
Unity, which never Fuses
Cross, which never Castigates

Heart, which never Forgets

EMBRACE

Enchanted to the memories unforgettable,
Mustering hopes to never fall apart.
Bonded with a sense of loyalty.
Reckoned to the thought another chance.
Alive after healing the deep wound.
Caressed every sweet moment.
Embraced all the negatives for another beginning.

TWENTY-TWO

HAIKU

A New Start

A new start,
Covenant of longing paved path,
Through painful tears.

♡♡♡

Enchanting Romance

Enticing Twilight
A least, enchanting romance
beyond the starlight

♡♡♡

Sand Castle

Shining summertime
A dreamy sand castle hides
enjoying the moment.

TWENTY-THREE

4 LINE POEM

Painful truth

I close my eyes to say hello.
Drops of tears on my pillow.
Agony, I can't get through.
Because that was the line I drew.

♡♡♡

Different ways

A promise that we made,
Broke it another day.
The second time was the chance.
Yet, you parted ways.

♡♡♡

Never-ending thoughts

Rising from her stiff bed,
Never-ending thoughts of sadness in her head,
She reveres being dead.
Enduring the day with endless dread.

♡♡♡

To Her

To her, it was a fairytale.
To her, it was to cover up the solitude.
To her, it was an incipient revelation of life.
To her, it was time to awake and face reality.

Printed by Libri Plureos GmbH in Hamburg, Germany